Y0-BEC-374

ALBERT EINSTEIN

FERNANDO GORDON

Consulting Editor, Diane Craig, M.A./Reading Specialist

Super Sandcastle

An Imprint of Abdo Publishing
abdopublishing.com

abdopublishing.com

THIS BOOK CONTAINS
RECYCLED MATERIALS

Editor: Rebecca Felix
Content Developer: Nancy Tuminelly
Cover and Interior Design and Production: Mighty Media, Inc.
Photo Credits: Doris Ulmann/Library of Congress; ETH-Bibliothek Zürich, Bildarchiv; Harris & Ewing/ Library of Congress; Orren Jack Turner/Library of Congress; Shutterstock; Wikimedia Commons

Library of Congress Cataloging-in-Publication Data
Names: Gordon, Fernando, author.
Title: Albert Einstein / by Fernando Gordon ; consulting editor, Diane Craig,
   M.A./reading specialist.
Description: Minneapolis, Minnesota : Abdo Publishing, [2017] | Series:
   Scientists at work
Identifiers: LCCN 2016001349 (print) | LCCN 2016009203 (ebook) | ISBN
   9781680781557 (print) | ISBN 9781680775983 (ebook)
Subjects: LCSH: Einstein, Albert, 1879-1955--Juvenile literature. |
   Physicists--Biography--Juvenile literature. | Nobel Prize
   winners--Biography--Juvenile literature.
Classification: LCC QC16.E5 G68 2017 (print) | LCC QC16.E5 (ebook) | DDC
   530.092--dc23
LC record available at http://lccn.loc.gov/2016001349

Super SandCastle™ books are created by a team of professional educators, reading specialists, and content developers around five essential components—phonemic awareness, phonics, vocabulary, text comprehension, and fluency—to assist young readers as they develop reading skills and strategies and increase their general knowledge. All books are written, reviewed, and leveled for guided reading, early reading intervention, and Accelerated Reader™ programs for use in shared, guided, and independent reading and writing activities to support a balanced approach to literacy instruction.

CONTENTS

A GREAT THINKER

Albert Einstein was a **physicist**. He came up with new ideas about space and time. He was an **activist** too. He was against war.

Albert Einstein

4

ALBERT EINSTEIN

BORN: March 14, 1879, Ulm, Germany

MARRIED: Mileva Maric (1903–1919), Elsa Löwenthal (1919–1936)

CHILDREN: Hans Albert, Eduard

DIED: April 18, 1955, Princeton, New Jersey

A CHILDHOOD OF WONDER

Albert was a curious child. His father gave him a compass when he was five. It amazed Albert. Why did the points move? He asked many questions.

Albert at age three

Albert grew up in Munich, Germany. School was hard for him. But a family friend helped Albert. Max Talmud often ate dinner with the Einsteins. He studied medicine. He taught Albert about science.

Albert with his younger sister, Maja

LIFE IN SWITZERLAND

Einstein's parents moved to Italy in 1894. Einstein stayed in Germany. He was supposed to finish school. Instead he dropped out.

Zurich, Switzerland

Einstein moved to Zurich, Switzerland. He finished school there in 1896. Then he went to the Swiss Federal Polytechnic School. He studied math and **physics**.

The Swiss Federal Polytechnic School

Einstein, 1896

MIRACLE YEAR

It was 1905. This is called Einstein's Miracle Year. He was living in Bern, Switzerland. He worked in a patent office. He studied **physics** in his free time.

Einstein, early 1900s

Einstein wrote several papers. He proved atoms exist. He also came up with a new **equation**. It was $E=mc^2$. It explained how matter turns into energy. He also came up with a **theory** about light. He said light was made of particles.

RELATIVITY

From 1905 to 1907 Einstein worked on an important idea. It was the **theory** of relativity. This is one of his most famous ideas. It says that the laws of **physics** are the same everywhere. It also says that light moves at a constant speed. But the way things appear to move depends on the viewer's position.

Einstein with his wife Mileva and their oldest son, Hans Albert

RISE TO FAME

At first scientists ignored Einstein. But soon his ideas were proven to be true. Einstein became famous. He gave speeches about his discoveries. He got a job at the Humboldt University of Berlin. He continued studying science.

Einstein taught physics at the Humboldt University of Berlin in Germany.

Einstein and Mileva divorced in 1919.
Later that year, Einstein married Elsa Löwenthal (left).

A NOBEL PRIZE

In 1921 Einstein won a **Nobel Prize**. It was for his work in **physics**. He became more famous than ever. Einstein spoke around the world. But Germany was dangerous in the 1930s. **Nazis** were capturing and killing Jewish people.

Einstein gave many speeches throughout his life.

Einstein was Jewish. His life was in danger. So, he and Elsa moved to the United States.

LIFE IN THE UNITED STATES

Einstein lived in Princeton, New Jersey. He taught **physics**. He kept studying science. He also worked for world peace. Scientists began using his **equation** to build a dangerous bomb. Einstein spoke against using the bomb.

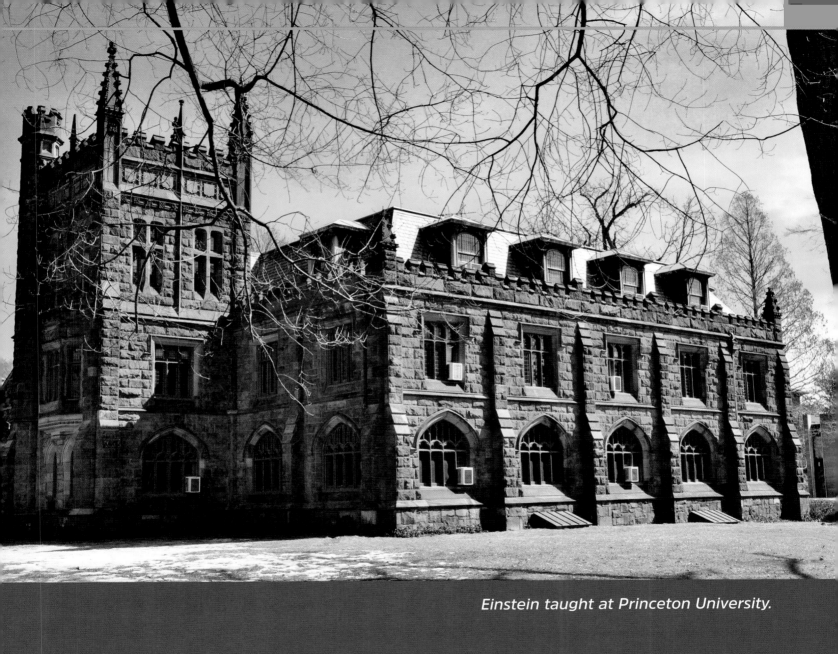

Einstein taught at Princeton University.

MOVING SCIENCE FORWARD

Einstein died in 1955. But his work was not forgotten. Einstein's **theories** changed the way we see the universe. They led to many more scientific discoveries.

A statue of Einstein in Washington, DC

MORE ABOUT EINSTEIN

Einstein played the VIOLIN.

Einstein was offered the PRESIDENCY of Israel. He turned it down.

Einstein said that the most important skills for kids were CARPENTRY and MUSIC!

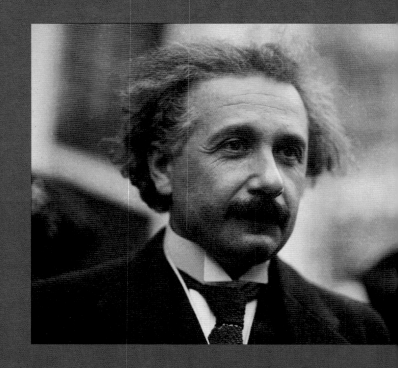

TEST YOUR KNOWLEDGE

1. How old was Einstein when he got a compass?

2. What is the name of the **theory** Einstein worked on from 1905 to 1907?

3. Einstein won a **Nobel Prize**.
True or false?

THINK ABOUT IT!

How do you use light every day?

ANSWERS: 1. Five 2. Theory of relativity 3. True

23

GLOSSARY

activist – a person who works for or against an issue.

equation – a number sentence in which the amounts on each side of the equal symbol name the same amount.

Nazi – a member of the political group that governed Germany from 1933–1945.

Nobel Prize – any of six yearly awards given for outstanding achievement in arts and sciences.

physics – the science of how energy and objects affect each other. Someone who studies physics is a physicist.

theory – an idea that explains how or why something happens.